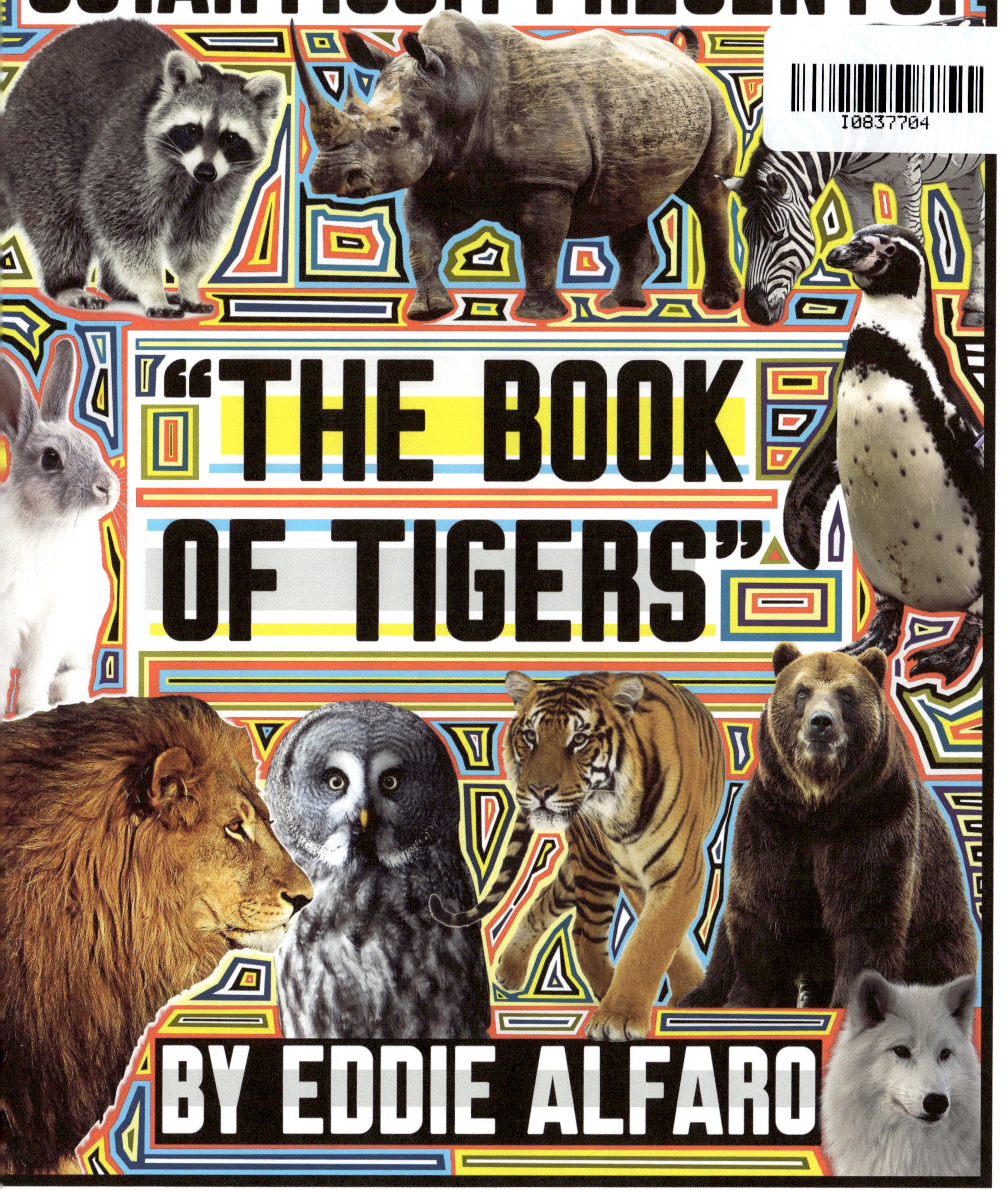

631ART.COM PRESENTS:
"THE BOOK OF TIGERS"
BY EDDIE ALFARO
I0837704

THE LATIN NAME FOR THE TIGER IS PANTHERA TIGRIS. THE WORD PANTHERA IS FROM THE GREEK WORD MEANING "HUNTER," WHILE TIGRIS IS AN OLD PERSIAN WORD MEANING "FAST" OR "ARROW-LIKE."

A TIGER'S TONGUE IS SO ROUGH THAT IT CAN SCRAPE THE MEAT OFF ITS PREY. IT'S SALIVA IS AN ANTISEPTIC. IT IS USEFUL FOR CLEANING THEIR WOUNDS.

THE TERM FOR A GROUP
OF TIGERS IS A "STREAK."

SIBERIAN TIGER
THE SIBERIAN TIGER IS THE BIGGEST OF ALL TIGERS.

TIGERS HAVE BEEN KNOWN TO IMITATE THE CALL OF OTHER ANIMALS TO SUCCESSFULLY ATTRACT PREY.

A TIGER SPENDS ABOUT 18 HOURS A DAY SLEEPING.

WHITE TIGERS CAN WEIGH UP TO AROUND 570 POUNDS, WHICH IS ABOUT THE WEIGHT OF TWO GIANT PANDAS.

THE TIGER IS THE NATIONAL ANIMAL
OF BOTH INDIA AND BANGLADESH.

A TIGER'S BACK LEGS ARE LONGER THAN ITS FRONT LEGS, WHICH MAKES IT GREAT AT RUNNING, JUMPING, AND POUNCING.

TIGERS ARE THE LARGEST CATS ON EARTH. THEY CAN WEIGH UP TO 720 POUNDS AND STRETCH 6 FEET LONG.

A TIGER'S PAW PRINT
IS CALLED A "PUG MARK."

A TIGER CAN EAT NEARLY 1/5 OF ITS BODY WEIGHT IN ONE MEAL.

A FULLY-GROWN
TIGER CAN LEAP
OVER 9 YARDS AND
JUMP UP TO 5
YARDS VERTICALLY.

TIGERS HAVE OVER 100 STRIPES, WHICH HELPS THE TIGER BLEND IN WITH LONG GRASS. LIKE FINGERPRINTS, NO TWO TIGERS HAVE THE SAME PATTERN.

A TIGER'S ROAR CAN BE
HEARD OVER 2 MILES
THROUGH A FOREST.

A TIGER'S CLAWS
CAN GROW UP TO
4.7 INCHES LONG.

WHITE BENGAL TIGERS ARE MOST LIKELY EXTINCT IN THE WILD, BUT THEY STILL LIVE IN ZOOS.

SUMATRAN TIGER
TIGERS LIKE TO BE NEAR WATER. THE SUMATRAN TIGER HAS WEBBED FEET, WHICH MAKES IT A VERY SKILLED SWIMMER.

INTERESTING FACTS ABOUT TIGERS:
MODERN TIGERS DID NOT DESCEND FROM PREHISTORIC SABER-TOOTH TIGERS. THE TWO ARE NOT CLOSELY RELATED.
TIGERS DO NOT LIVE IN AFRICA.
A TIGER'S TAIL HELPS IT BALANCE WHILE ITS RUNNING. ITS TAIL CAN BE UP TO ONE-THIRD OF ITS BODY LENGTH.
A TIGER'S NIGHT VISION IS 6 TIMES BETTER THAN A HUMAN'S.

THE EARLIEST TIGER FOSSILS ARE 2 MILLION YEARS OLD.
TIGERS CANNOT PURR. WHEN THEY ARE HAPPY OR FEEL SAFE, THEY SQUINT OR CLOSE THEIR EYES.
EACH TIGER HAS ITS OWN SCENT DUE TO INDIVIDUALIZED SCENT GLANDS.
TIGERS HAVE THE LARGEST BRAIN OF ANY CARNIVORE, EXCEPT THE POLAR BEAR.

THANK YOU.
THE END.

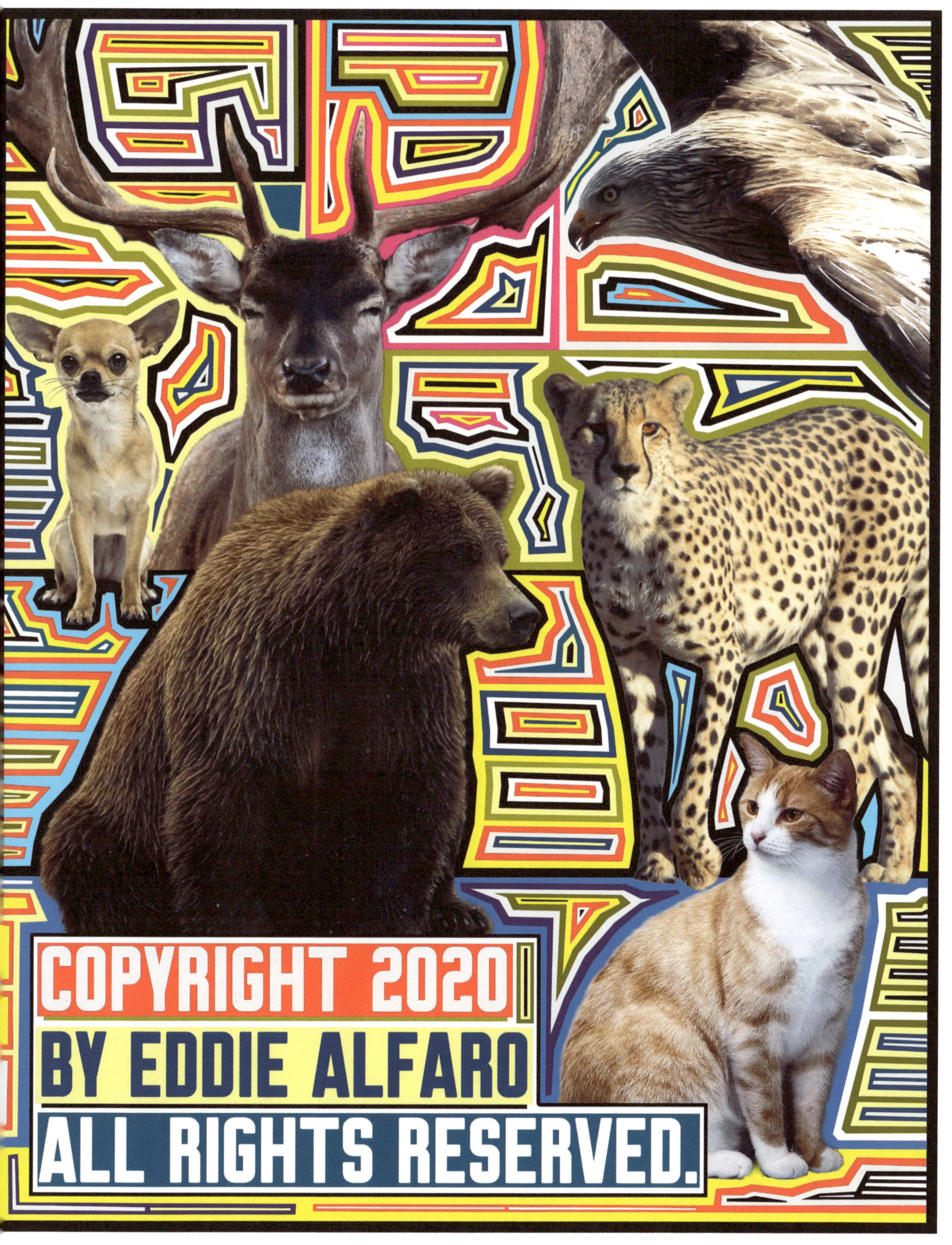
COPYRIGHT 2020
BY EDDIE ALFARO
ALL RIGHTS RESERVED.

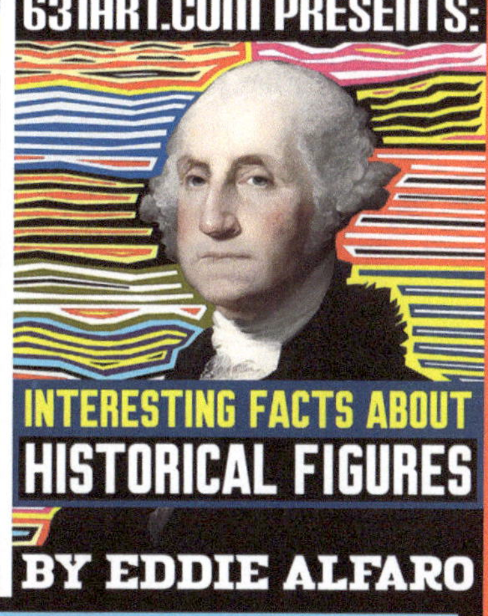

MORE BOOKS AT:

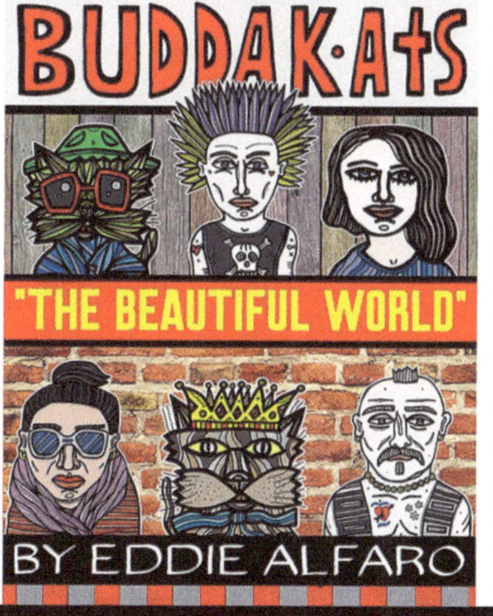

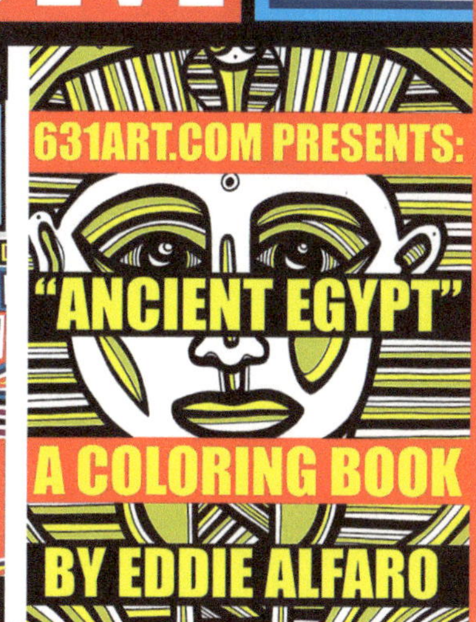